PIANO · VOCAL · GUITAR

BURLESQUE:
MUSIC FROM THE MOTION PICTURE SOUNDTRACK

ISBN 978-1-61780-322-2

HAL•LEONARD®
CORPORATION
7777 W. BLUEMOUND RD. P.O. BOX 13819 MILWAUKEE, WI 53213

Visit Hal Leonard Online at
www.halleonard.com

Due to licensing restrictions, "But I Am a Good Girl" is not included in this folio.

SOMETHING'S GOT A HOLD ON ME

Words and Music by ETTA JAMES,
LEROY KIRKLAND and PEARL WOODS

Oh, _____ some - times, _____ I get a good feel - ing, yeah. _____

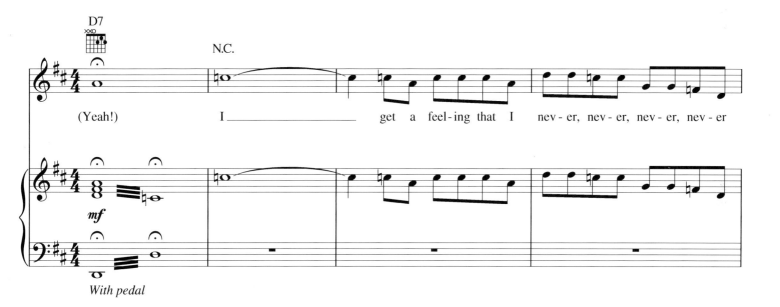

(Yeah!) I _____ get a feel - ing that I nev - er, nev - er, nev - er, nev - er

With pedal

had be - fore, _____ no, no. _____ (Yeah!) I _____ just got - ta

Recorded a half step lower.

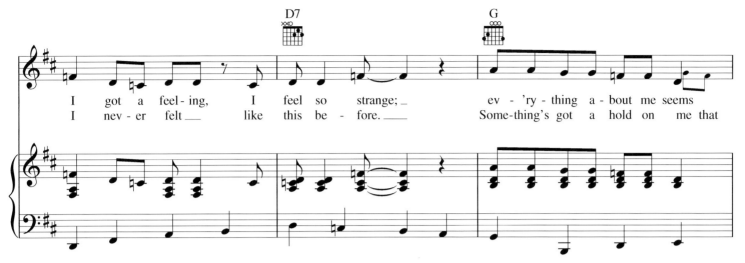

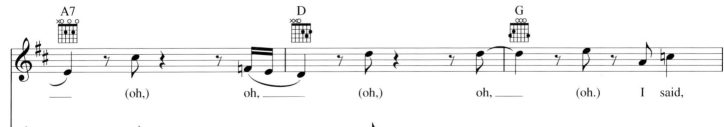

WELCOME TO BURLESQUE

Words and Music by CHARLIE MIDNIGHT,
MATTHER GERRARD, STEVE LINDSEY
and JOHN SHANLEY

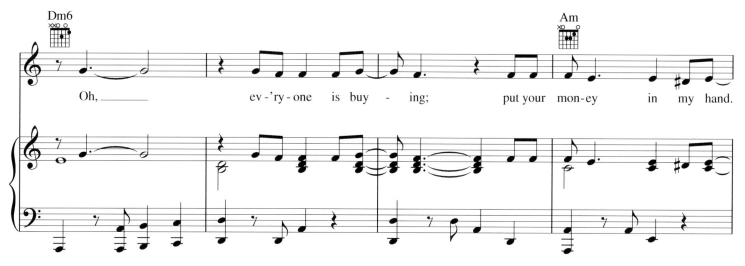

Oh, _____ ev-'ry-one is buy - ing; put your mon-ey in my hand.

If you've got a lit - tle ex - tra, well, *(Spoken:) give it to the band.*

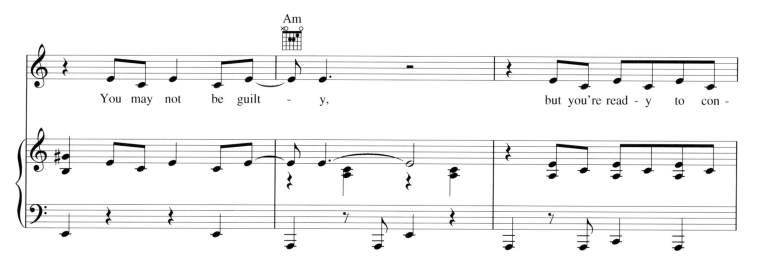

You may not be guilt - y, but you're read - y to con -

guess - ing, so cool __ and stat - u - esque. __

"Be-have your-self," says Geor - gia; __ wel - come __ to Bur - lesque.

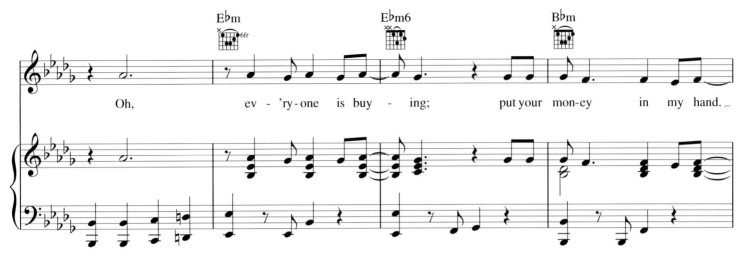

Oh, ev-'ry-one is buy - ing; put your mon-ey in my hand. _

If you want a lit - tle ex - tra, _____ well,

(Spoken:) you know where I am. Some-thing ver - y dark _____

is play - ing with your mind. _ It's not the end of days, _

it's just the bump and grind.

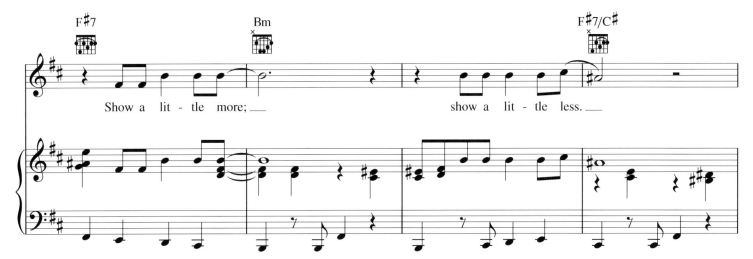

Show a lit - tle more; ___ show a lit - tle less. ___

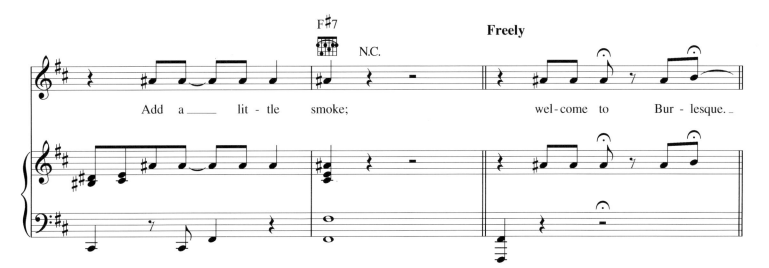

Add a ___ lit - tle smoke; wel - come to Bur - lesque. ___

TOUGH LOVER

Words and Music by ETTA JAMES
and JOE JOSEA

yeah yeah __ yeah. __ A tough lov - er, yeah, yeah. __ Yeah,

when he kiss - es me, I get that thrill. __ When he do the wig - gle, I won't __

Bright Shuffle

__ keep still. __ I want a tough lov - er, yeah, yeah. __

Tough lov - er, whoo. __ I need a tough lov - er,

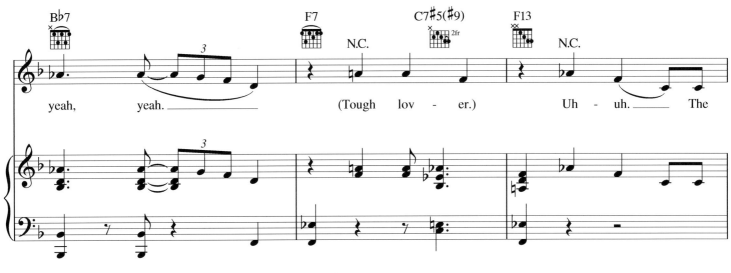

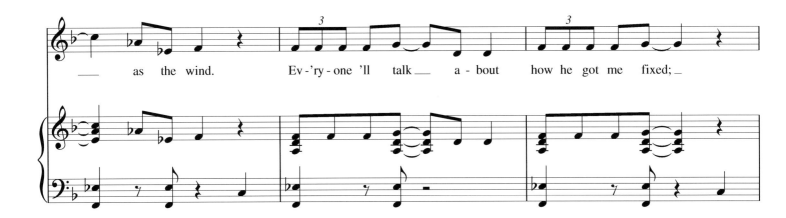

er come to pass.___ Don Juan ain't___ got half____ the chance.___ He's a

tough lov - er, yeah, yeah._____ Tough lov - er, whoo.__

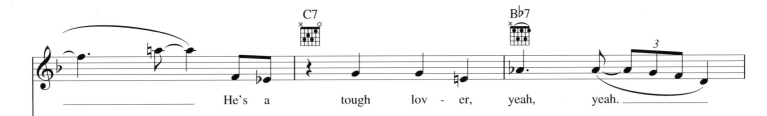

_____ He's a tough lov - er, yeah, yeah._____

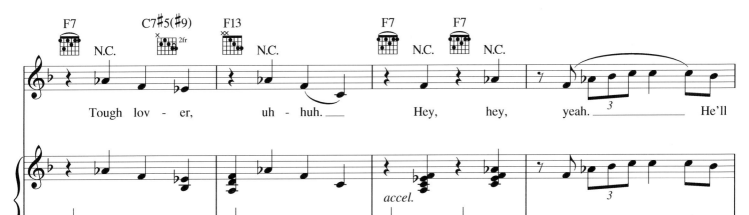

Tough lov - er, uh - huh.__ Hey, hey, yeah._____ He'll

A GUY WHAT TAKES HIS TIME

Words and Music by
RALPH RAINGER

Slow Blues

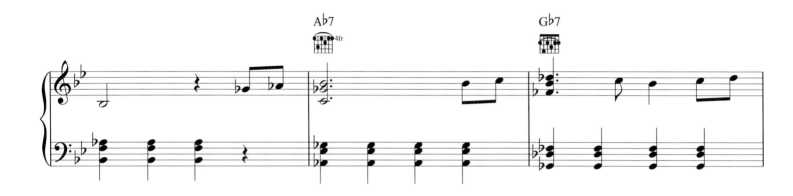

A

de - mon for slow mo - tion or such. _____ Why should
ate a con - nois - seur _____ in trade _____ who would

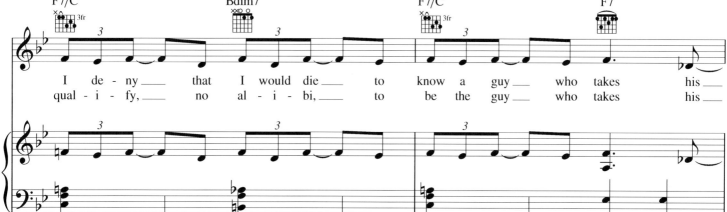

I de - ny _____ that I would die _____ to know a guy _____ who takes his _____
qual - i - fy, _____ no al - i - bi, _____ to be the guy _____ who takes his _____

_____ time? _____ There _____ time? _____

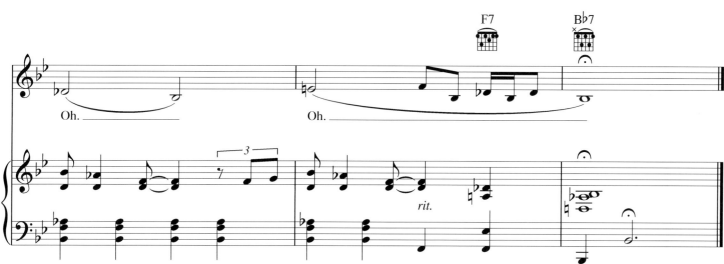

Oh. _____ Oh. _____

rit.

EXPRESS

Words and Music by CHRISTINA AGUILERA,
CHRISTOPHER STEWART and CLAUDE KELLY

Recorded a half step lower.

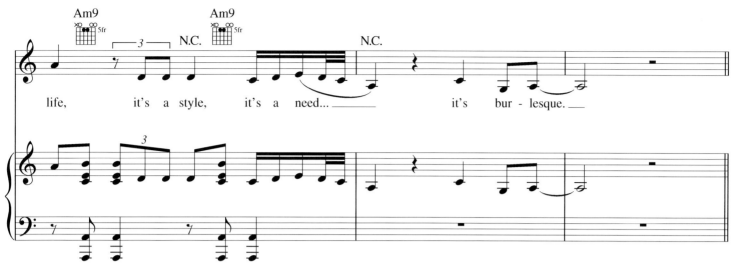

life,   it's a style,   it's a need... _____   it's   bur - lesque. _____

Techno groove (♪♪ = ♪♪)

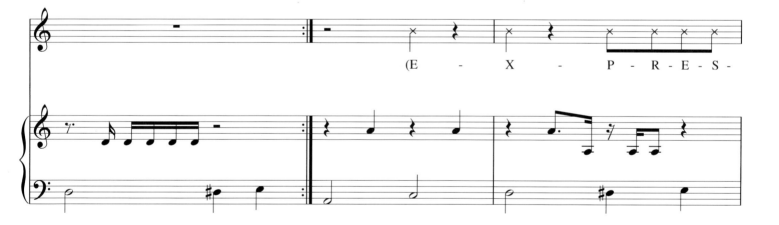

(E - X - P - R - E - S-

S;   love,   sex,   la - dies, no re - grets.   E -

got that cer - tain *sav - oir - faire,_____ eh. (Fas -
pleas - ure brings them to their knees,_____ hey.

ten up; can you im - ag - ine what would hap-pen if I let you close e-nough to touch?

Step in - to the fan - tas - y; you'll nev - er want ___ to leave, ba - by, that's guar - an - teed.) (Why?)

It's a pas - sion, an e - mo - tion; it's a fash - ion....___ (Bur - lesque.)

D.S. al Coda

CODA

it? ____ (It's bur - lesque.)

(Bur - lesque.)

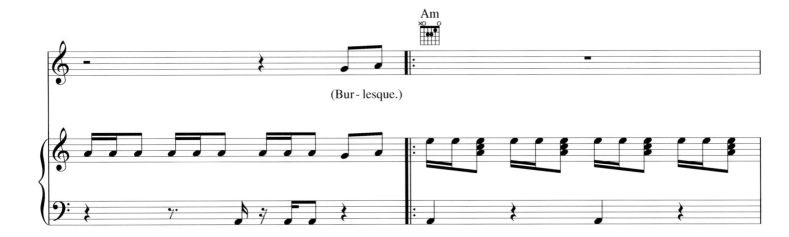

Am

(Bur - lesque.)

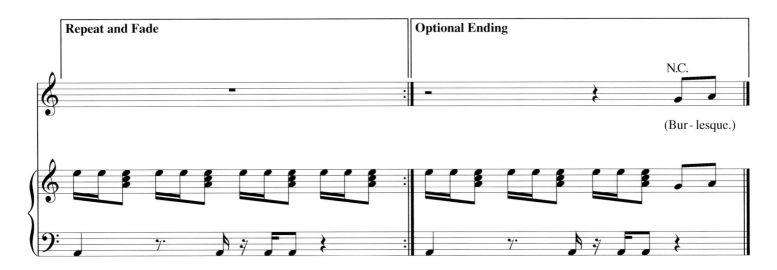

Repeat and Fade

Optional Ending

N.C.

(Bur - lesque.)

YOU HAVEN'T SEEN THE LAST OF ME

Words and Music by
DIANE WARREN

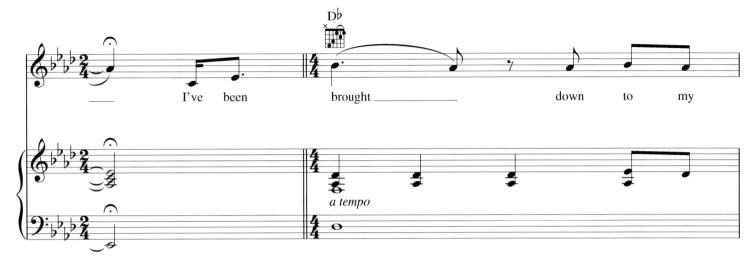

I've been brought _____ down to my

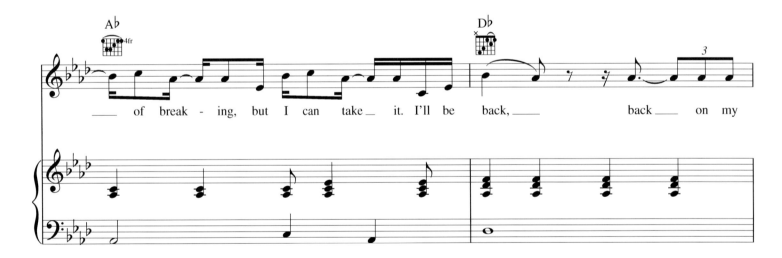

knees. And I've been pushed _____ way past _____ the point _____

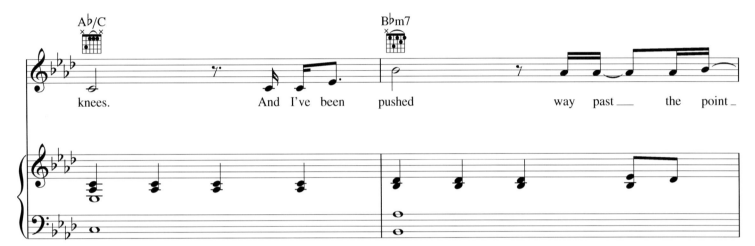

_____ of break - ing, but I can take _____ it. I'll be back, _____ back _____ on my

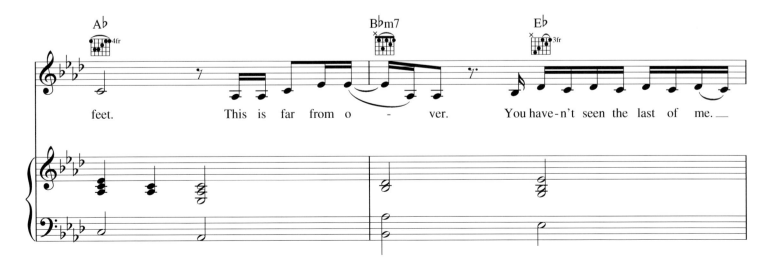

feet. This is far from o - ver. You have-n't seen the last of me. _____

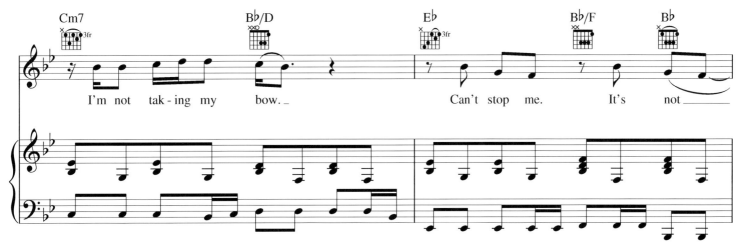

I'm not tak-ing my bow. ___ Can't stop me. It's not ___

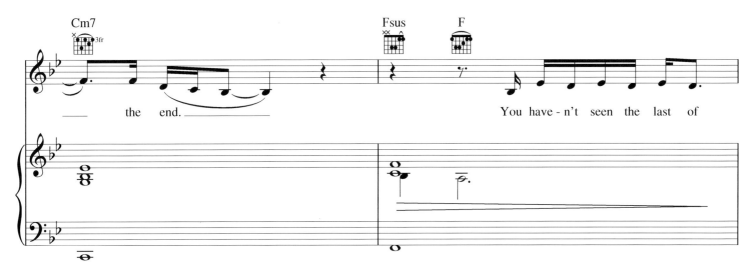

___ the end. ___ You have-n't seen the last of

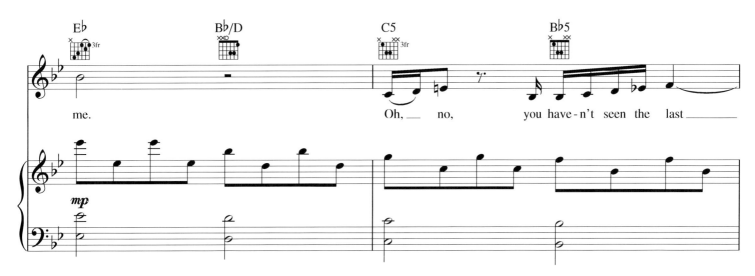

me. Oh, ___ no, you have-n't seen the last ___

___ of me. You have-n't seen the last ___ of me. ___

BOUND TO YOU

Words and Music by CHRISTINA AGUILERA,
SIA FURLER and SAMUEL DIXON

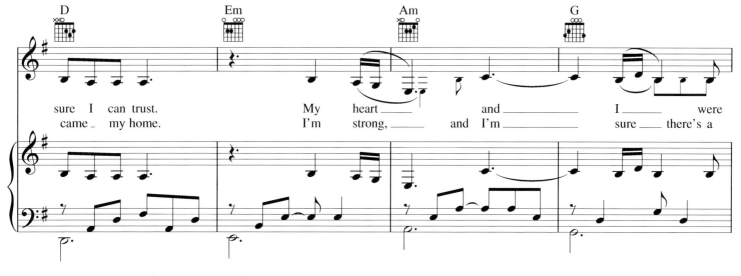

sure I can trust. My heart ___ and ___ I ___ were
came _ my home. I'm strong, ___ and I'm ___ sure ___ there's a

bur-ied in dust. Free me, ___ free ___ us. ___
fire _ in us. Sweet love, ___ so ___ pure. ___

___ You're all ___ I need ___ when I'm
___ I catch ___ my breath; ___ we're just

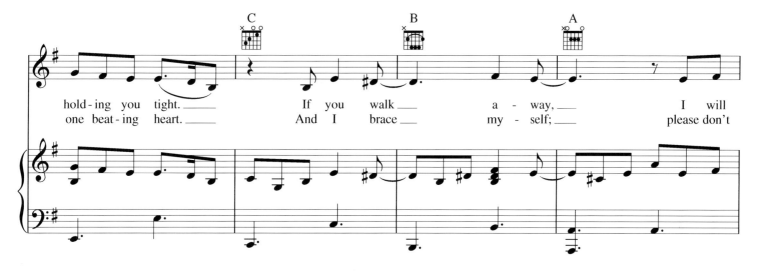

hold-ing you tight. ___ If you walk ___ a - way, ___ I will
one beat-ing heart. ___ And I brace ___ my - self; ___ please don't

suf - fer to - night. _____ I found a man I can trust; _
tear this a - part. _____

and boy, I be - lieve in us. _____ I am

ter - ri - fied _____ to love for the first time. _____

Can't you see that I'm bound in chains? _____ I

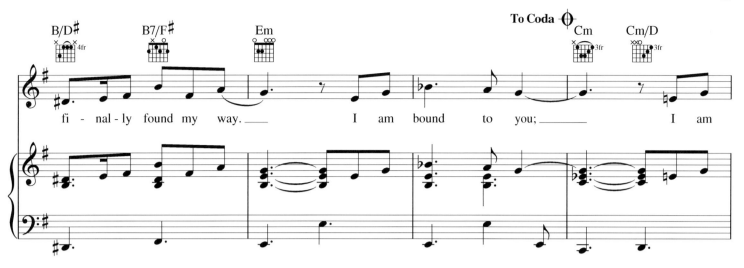

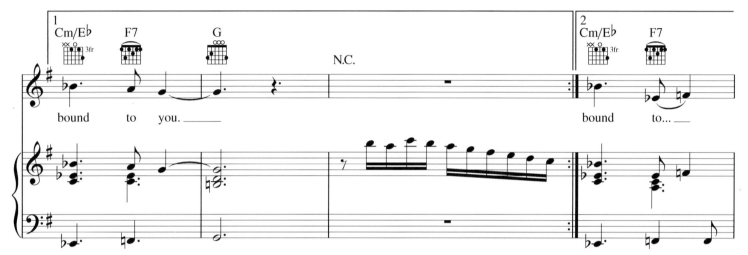

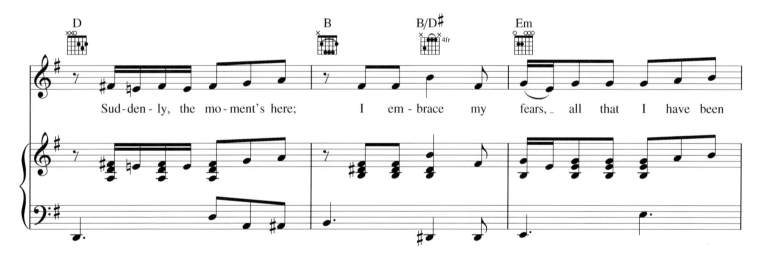

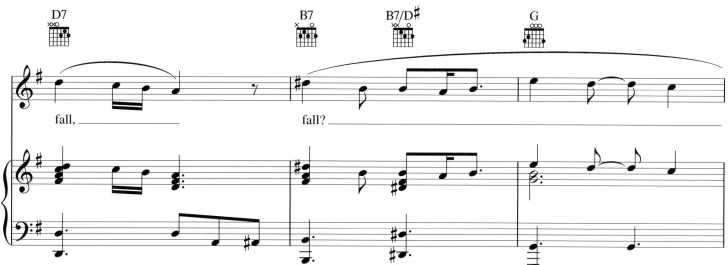

fall, _____ _____ fall? _____

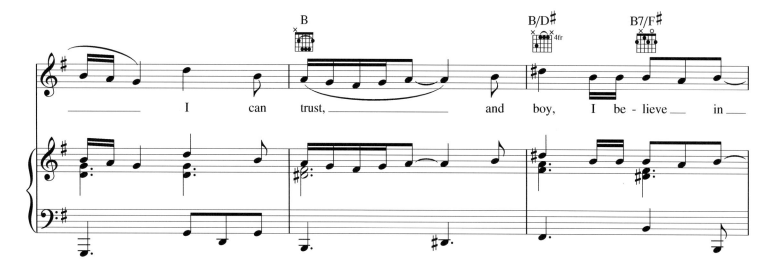

_____ I can trust, _____ and boy, I be-lieve __ in __

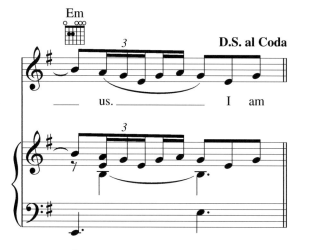

_____ us. _____ I am

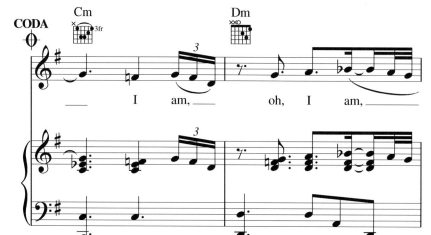

I am, _____ oh, I am, _____

__ I'm bound _____ to _____ you. _____

SHOW ME HOW YOU BURLESQUE

Words and Music by CHRISTINA AGUILERA,
CHRISTOPHER STEWART and CLAUDE KELLY

ooh, ooh.) (Wah ooh, ooh.)

ba - by doll just comes to life _____ un - der the
ev - 'ry - bod - y just comes to life _____ un - der the

(Wah ooh, ooh.)

spot - light. _____ All the girls wan - na fall in line. _____
spot - light. _____ All the boys wan - na fall be - hind. _____

(We say:)

Yeah. _____ (Here ___ come the la - dies, 'bout to

give a lit - tle show.) Yeah. _____ (Here ___ go the boys, are yell - ing,

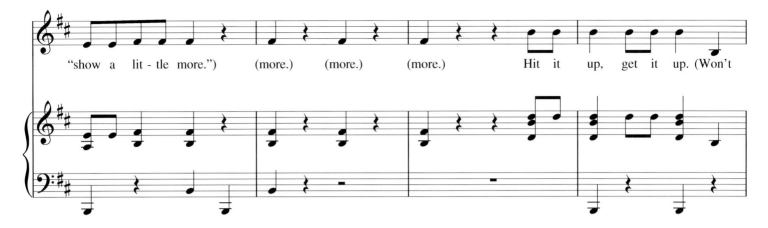

"show a lit-tle more.") (more.) (more.) (more.) Hit it up, get it up. (Won't

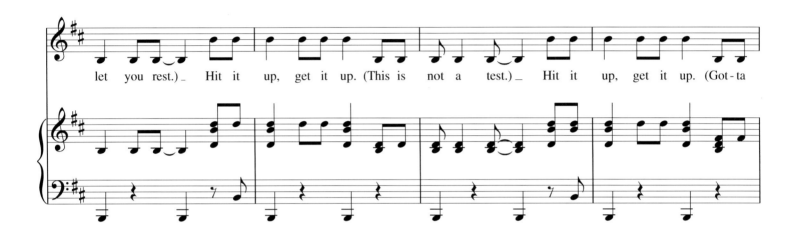

let you rest.)_ Hit it up, get it up. (This is not a test.)_ Hit it up, get it up. (Got-ta

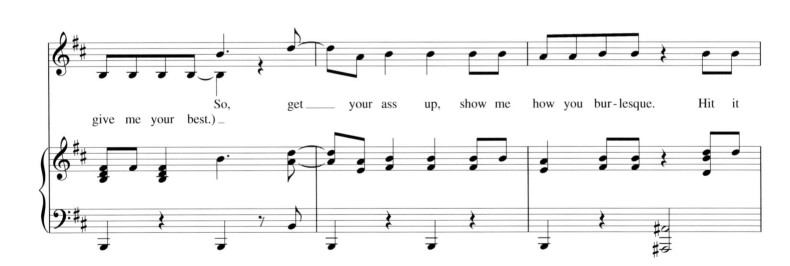

So, get___ your ass up, show me how you bur-lesque. Hit it

give me your best.)_

up, get it up. (Won't let you rest.)_ Hit it up, get it up. (This is not a test.)_ Hit it

To Coda ⊕

up, get it up. (Got - ta give me your best.) ___ So, get ___ your ass up, show me

how you bur-lesque.

(A lit - tle bit of naught-y, it's a lit - tle bit nice. She's a whole lot - ta glam, sweat,

sug - ar, sex, spice. Just shim - my, shim - my, strut, strut, give a lit - tle what, what. Up

THE BEAUTIFUL PEOPLE
(From Burlesque)

Words and Music by MARILYN MANSON, TWIGGY RAMIREZ,
RONALD FAIR, NICOLE SCHERZINGER,
ESTHER DEAN, STEFANIE RIDEL,
LAURA PERGOLIZZI, MELVIN K. WATSON, JR.,
LARRY SUMMERVILLE, JR. and TOMMY LEE JAMES

* *Recorded a half step higher.*

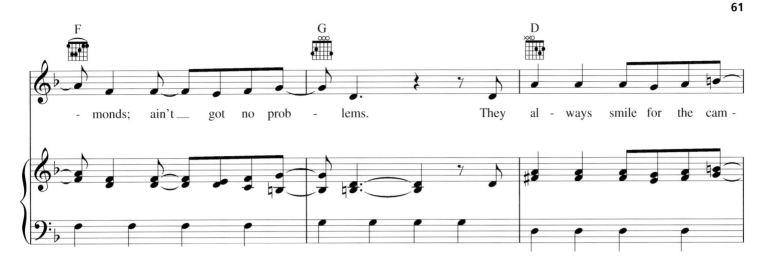

-monds; ain't__ got no prob - lems. They al - ways smile for the cam-

-'ra, steal - ing the spot - light, liv - ing the high - life._____ 'Cause it's the

beau - ti - ful beau - ti - ful beau - ti - ful beau - ti - ful peo - ple they want, __ and it's the

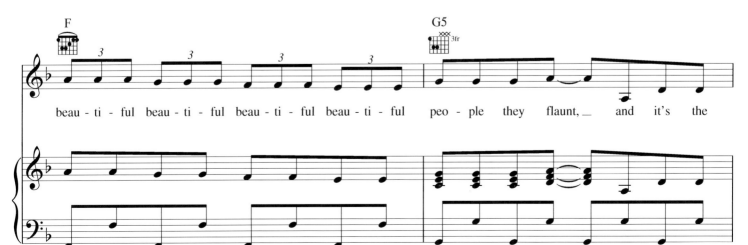

beau - ti - ful beau - ti - ful beau - ti - ful beau - ti - ful peo - ple they flaunt, __ and it's the

be just like _____ you, _____ one of the

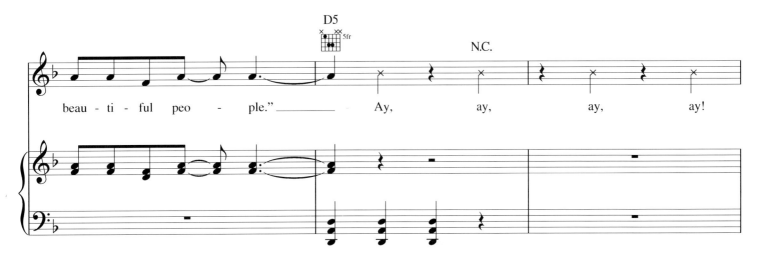

beau - ti - ful peo - ple." _____ Ay, ay, ay, ay!

(The beau - ti - ful peo - ple, the beau - ti - ful peo - ple, _____ ah.)

(The beau - ti - ful peo - ple, the beau - ti - ful peo - ple.) _____

It's the beau - ti - ful peo - ple, _____

(The beau-ti-ful peo-ple, the beau-ti-ful peo-ple.) __ hey, __

__ the beau-ti-ful peo-ple they love. __ Hey, __ yeah. __

D(add2)   Am7   F

(All of the beau-ti-ful peo-ple; wan-na be, don't you

G   D(add2)

wan-na be like all of the beau-ti-ful peo-

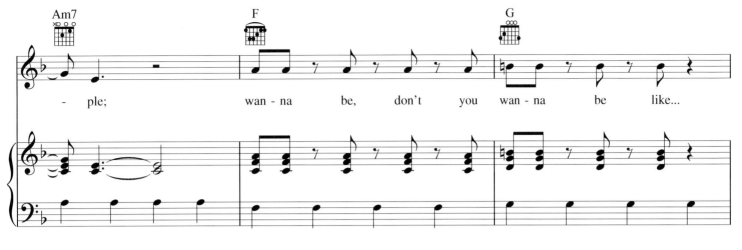

- ple; wan - na be, don't you wan - na be like...

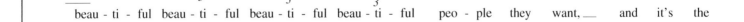

Hey!
Oh.) _____ Beau - ti - ful peo - ple they love. ___
'Cause it's the

beau - ti - ful beau - ti - ful beau - ti - ful beau - ti - ful peo - ple they want, ___ and it's the

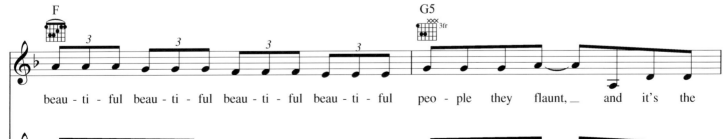

beau - ti - ful beau - ti - ful beau - ti - ful beau - ti - ful peo - ple they flaunt, ___ and it's the

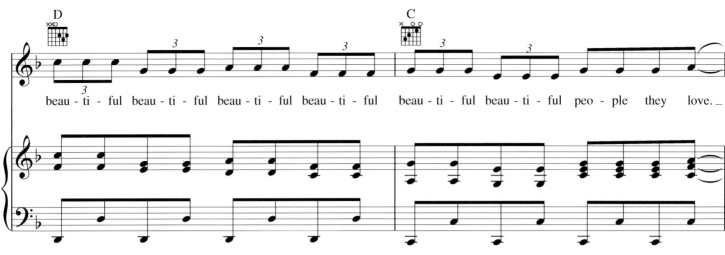

beau - ti - ful beau - ti - ful beau - ti - ful beau - ti - ful   beau - ti - ful beau - ti - ful peo - ple they love. ___

_____   'Cause it's the ___   Yeah. ___

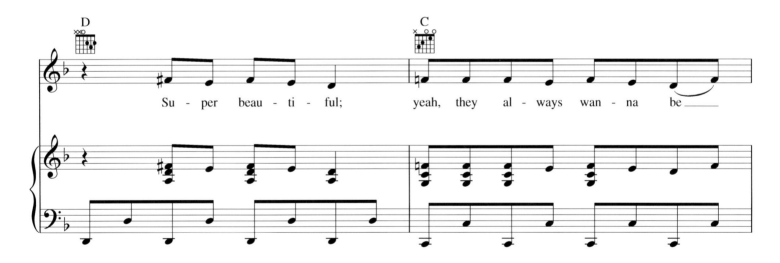

Su - per beau - ti - ful;   yeah, they al - ways wan - na be _____

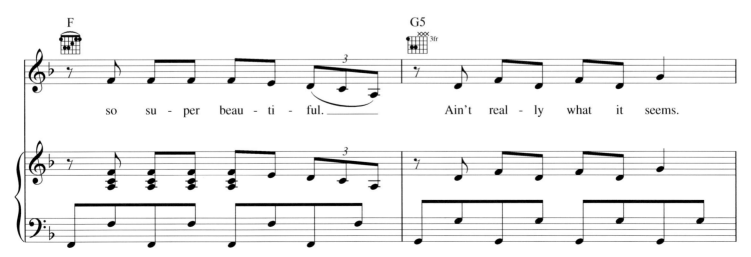

so su - per beau - ti - ful. _____   Ain't real - ly what it seems.

Ev - 'ry - bod - y wants it, ev - 'ry - bod - y wants a piece ____

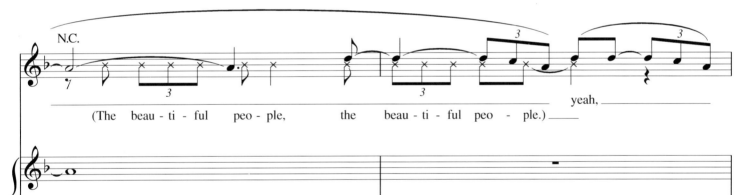

of su - per beau - ti - ful. ____ They all wan - na be, ____

N.C.

(The beau - ti - ful peo - ple, the beau - ti - ful peo - ple.) ____ yeah, ____

yeah. ____ (The beau - ti - ful peo - ple, the beau - ti - ful peo - ple.) ____

DIAMONDS ARE A GIRL'S BEST FRIEND

Words by LEO ROBIN
Music by JULE STYNE

Bright Shuffle

2nd time Instrumental solo

kiss on the hand may be quite con - ti - nen - tal, but

dia - monds are a girl's best friend. A

kiss may be grand, ___ but it won't pay the rent - al on your

hum - ble flat, or help you at the au - to - mat.

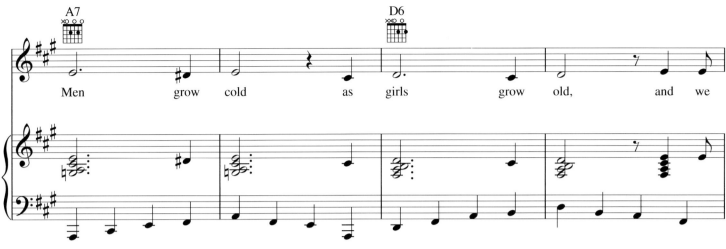

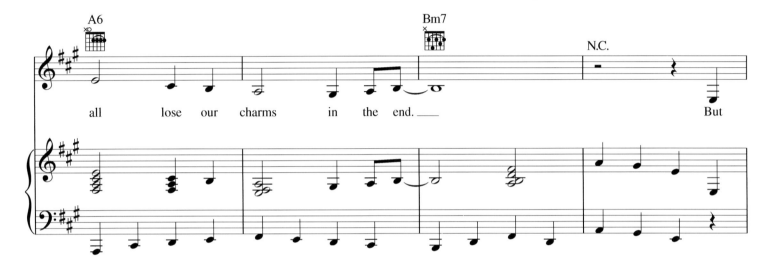

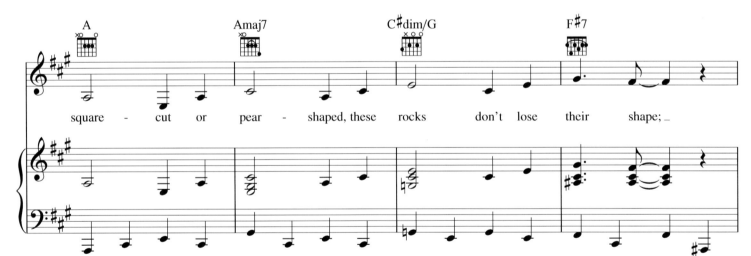

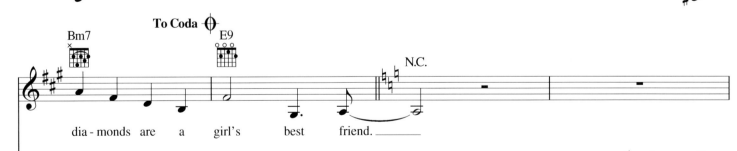

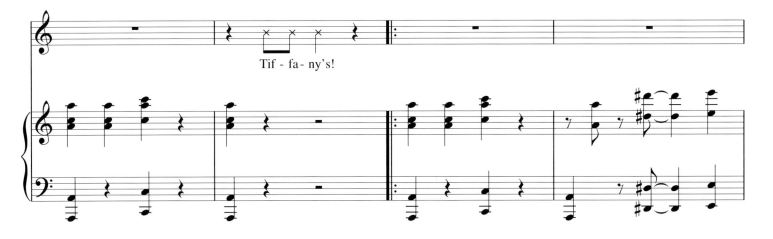

Tif - fa - ny's!

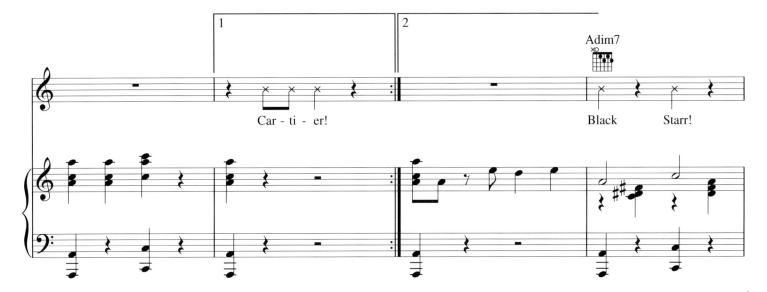

1 Car - ti - er!

2 Adim7 Black Starr!

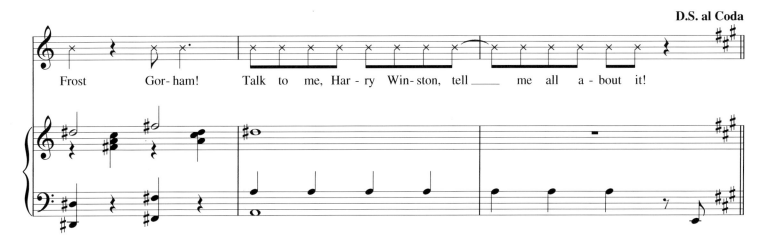

D.S. al Coda

Frost Gor - ham! Talk to me, Har - ry Win - ston, tell ___ me all a - bout it!

CODA E9 N.C.

Solo ends I've heard of af - fairs that are

strict - ly pla - ton - ic, but dia - monds are a girl's __ best

friend. And I ___ think af - fairs that you

must keep liai - son - ic are bet - ter bets if

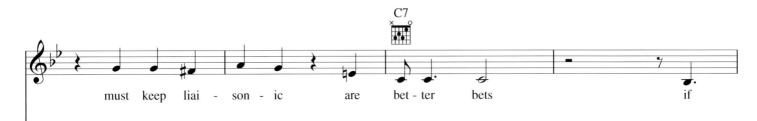

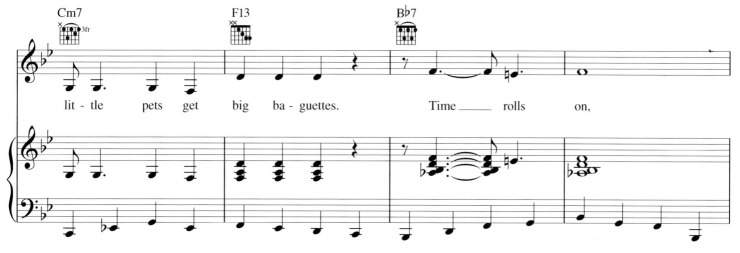

little pets get big baguettes. Time _____ rolls on,

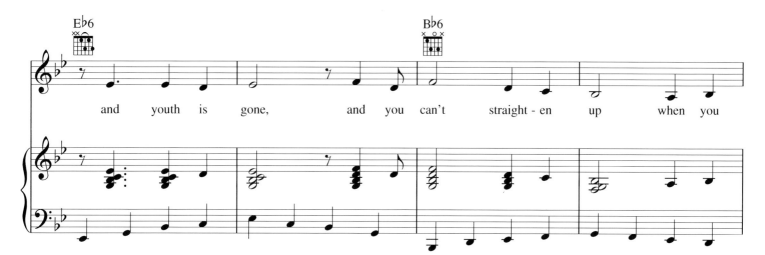

and youth is gone, and you can't straighten up when you

bend. But stiff back or stiff knees, you

stand straight at Tiff - 'ny's. Dia - monds! _____

LONG JOHN BLUES

Words and Music by
TOMMY GEORGE

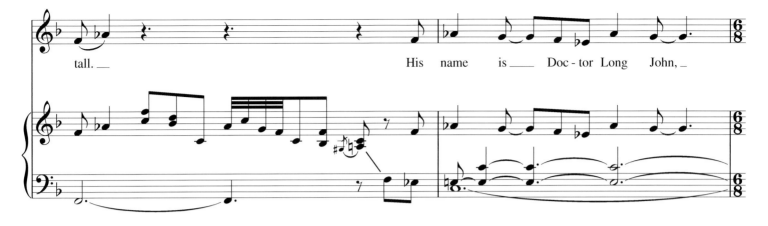

tall. ___ His name is ___ Doc - tor Long John, ___

and he an - swers ev -'ry call.

Slow Blues

You know, ___

I went to Long John's of - fice; I said, "Doc - tor, the pain ___ is ___

kill - ing __ me." Ooh, __ I _____ went to Long John's of - fice; I said,

"Doc - tor, the pain _____ is _____ kill - ing me." He said,

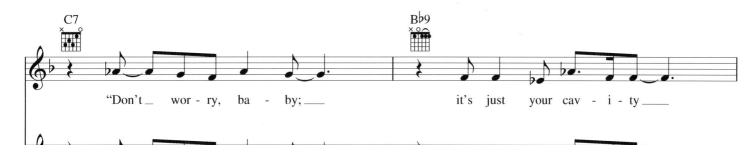

"Don't __ wor - ry, ba - by; ___ it's just your cav - i - ty ___

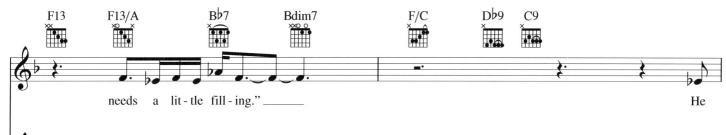

needs a lit - tle fill - ing." _____ He

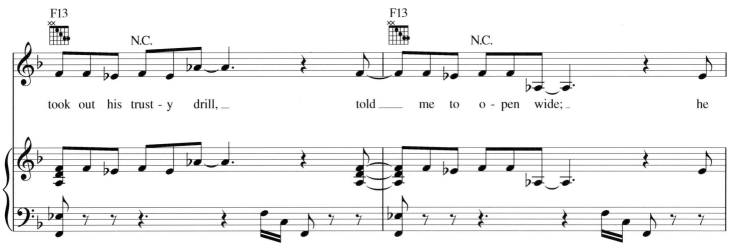

took out his trust-y drill, __ told __ me to o - pen wide; __ he

said it would-n't hurt me; then he filled my whole in - side. __

__ Oh, Je - sus, Long John, __ don't you nev - er go a - way; __

'cause you thrill me __ when you drill me, __ and